# BITCOIN
# Vs.
# ETHEREUM

Cryptocurrency Investing Tips
You Wish You Knew

## Table of Contents

Preface .................................................................................................. 5

Introduction ........................................................................................ 7

Chapter 1: What Are The Differences Between Bitcoin And Ethereum ............................................................................................. 9

Chapter 2: Opportunities To Invest In Bitcoin (Classic And Cash) Vs. Ethereum ........................................................................ 18

Chapter 3: The Rules Of Serious Investing ................................. 39

Chapter 4: How To Reduce Your Risks With These Investments ............................................................................................................. 46

Chapter 5: Best Strategies For Mid- And Long-Term Success With Cryptocurrency Investing ..................................................... 54

Conclusion ......................................................................................... 59

© Copyright 2017 by Chad B. Harper - All rights reserved.

The following eBook is reproduced below with the goal of providing information that is as accurate and reliable as possible. Regardless, purchasing this eBook can be seen as consent to the fact that both the publisher and the author of this book are in no way experts on the topics discussed within and that any recommendations or suggestions that are made herein are for entertainment purposes only. Professionals should be consulted as needed prior to undertaking any of the action endorsed herein.

This declaration is deemed fair and valid by both the American Bar Association and the Committee of Publishers Association and is legally binding throughout the United States.

Furthermore, the transmission, duplication or reproduction of any of the following work including specific information will be considered an illegal act irrespective of if it is done electronically or in print. This extends to creating a secondary or tertiary copy of the work or a recorded copy and is only allowed with express written consent of the Publisher. All additional right reserved.

The information in the following pages is broadly considered to be a truthful and accurate account of facts and as such any inattention, use or misuse of the information in question by the reader will render any resulting actions solely under their purview. There are no scenarios in which the publisher or the original author of this work can be in any fashion deemed liable for any hardship or damages that may befall them after undertaking information described herein.

Additionally, the information in the following pages is intended only for informational purposes and should thus be thought of as universal. As befitting its nature, it is presented without assurance regarding its prolonged validity or interim quality. Trademarks that are mentioned are done without written consent and can in no way be considered an endorsement from the trademark holder.

# Preface

Cryptocurrency, Bitcoin, Ethereum and the like are heavily used buzz words today. Though not existing some years ago and also not known by majority of people when they were born, these terms become popular in very short time. All media, online or traditional are now full of it and are generating a never-ending news stream around this subject. Above all because they are attached to the opportunity of making money, these terms turned into synonyms for profits like those in the old days of the gold rush. Subsequent to this phenomenon an abundance of information related to these topics is popping up like mushrooms in a forest after a heavy rain. Despite this fact the author could only find books either focusing on the one or the other technology but none comparing the two most important of the currently available cryptocurrencies: Bitcoin and Ether (based on Ethereum technology). Especially from the perspective of an investor who wants to make educated decisions. This was the main reason for him to write this book and give a guideline also to others with this specific need.

While the book contains useful information for the serious investors it is not a how-to-get-rich-quick guideline. Sure, there are boat loads of profits one could make with these new opportunities out there. However, on the opposite you could also lose your shirt very easily if you're not aware of the downsides and traps and don't apply a sound strategy.

This book is subsequently focusing on a long-term investing approach. It can be useful to find a very own strategy related to investments in Bitcoin and/or Ethereum for sustainable profits. But this book is not written for „gamblers" who are just out for speculation and behind the quick win with these digital assets.

Furthermore considering the very nature of the books subject some specific information provided in the book will get outdated when short term developments are taking place after publishing date. The author will therefore update the content accordingly in the following editions.

# Introduction

Investing is an awesome approach to enable your cash to expand for you. At the same time as loads of individuals simply work their own particular occupations and expect that will be sufficient to pay the bills every month, savvy speculators can put their reserve funds and their cash to work, increasing it in means that numerous individuals just contemplate. There are many choices with regards to investing, yet one of the up-and-coming markets that is doing great is in cryptocurrency.

Investing into cryptographic money can be exceptionally confounding as it contrasts altogether from how one would come up to stocks. Purchasing Bitcoin (BTC) or Ether isn't like purchasing shares; instead, you are obtaining digital tokens that have specific functionalities, for example, a decentralized, pseudo-anonymous currency for Bitcoin's instance or fuel for decentralized apps & smart contracts for the Ethereum (ETH) platform. You anticipate adoption and technological developments to decode to claim for your coins/tokens and subsequently return on your investment. A number of exceptionally ambitious financial specialists will even trade cryptocurrency pairs, for example, BTC/ETH or BTC/LTC (Litecoin).

It's 2017 and the cryptocurrency festivity is prospering ahead with both Bitcoin plus Ethereum up 400% & 5000% at one point correspondingly. Banks took an enormous U-turn and stopped shutting down the accounts of alleged suspicious Bitcoin dealers for joining the Ethereum Enterprise Alliance. However, in the midst of this protruding setting or bubble contingent upon your perspective, there are shockingly not very many direct, end-to-end assets for the retail investor to partake in this conjecture smorgasbord.

Cryptocurrency supporters probably trusted it was inevitable. While boundless adoption of digital currencies as investment vehicles have by and large been moderate, especially among customary money related organizations, various well-known rich people have as of late done the swap far from more established methods of investment. A report proposes that the billionaires originate from inside and outside of the cryptocurrency space, comprising high up names such as Kik founder & CEO Ted Livingston, investment guru Tim Draper, Michael Novogratz, the major hedge fund player, together with entrepreneur Mark Cuban.

*Could this flag a more extensive move in the direction of crypto-currencies as investment alternatives? The world has to wait & watch!*

In this book, we will examine more on this and include a few other vital aspects regarding cryptocurrency investment, for example, the best possible & most secure approach to take an interest in the cryptocurrency market, how to settle on smart investment choices with BTC/ETH, how to lessen the risks & complexities of cryptocurrency investment, as well as a few methodologies/proposals and effective tips & tricks in the least difficult way imaginable.

While there is an abundance of information out there, some which is to a great degree technical, the procedure itself is in reality truly straightforward. Try not to give alien jargon and terminology a chance to drive you away!

# CHAPTER 1:

# What are the Differences Between Bitcoin and Ethereum

Cryptocurrency has changed a lot over the past few years. What started out as a simple idea to purchase items online has grown all over the world. People use bitcoins to purchase items while keeping their identities safe (much better than using your credit card and keeping all that personal information out there), but there are other ways to use this as well. Cryptocurrency has grown to include investing, selling items, making an income, and even backing up new start-up businesses. It is a whole new world of currency and many people want to learn how to take advantage of it.

Cryptocurrency, even though it is a newer idea, is still a form of money. For some people, that is all they need to know about it. There are a few stores who will accept cryptocurrency (it can be converted to American dollars as well as to some other currencies in some countries), as long as you have the right barcodes to make this happen. But for the most part, cryptocurrency is used and traded online.

Currently there are many different types of cryptocurrencies available. Bitcoin is probably one of the best known, but each of them will have their own value and it does go up and down a bit depending on the market. The Bitcoin right now is worth about $3,461 (Jul 23, 2017) American dollars, but other cryptocurrencies may be worth more or less depending on how many people are using them. These currencies are often considered stronger than regular currency, though, since they won't be tied to a bank or a government.

The biggest difference between cryptocurrencies and regular money from the bank is that these cryptocurrencies are not going to be backed by the government. The cryptocurrencies are going to have rules that were programmed into them and this will control how they work, rather than the government. Some people prefer this method because they don't have to worry about the government meddling in the value of their money.

All cryptocurrencies are going to be based on technology that includes data verification and advanced encryption, which helps to keep them secure and makes it hard for someone to forge the currency. In addition, these currencies are often designed with a specific maximum amount of currency available so inflation will stay pretty steady over time.

Now, there are going to be some differences between the cryptocurrencies, including who uses them, how they are designed, and how much currency is available, but they can often come from the same basis and will be used by consumers in the same way. This guidebook is going to focus on two of the big names in cryptocurrencies; Bitcoin and Ethereum.

## The basics of Bitcoin

Let's start with Bitcoin. This is for sure the most popular cryptocurrency. It is used to pay for things, but like the other cryptocurrencies, it is not tied to a government or a bank. This type of cryptocurrency is going to work like a big ledger that

*Chapter 1: What are the Differences Between Bitcoin and Ethereum*

all of the users are able to share. When you get paid or pay for something using the Bitcoin system, all of these transactions are going to be placed on a ledger. Computers will then compete with each other to confirm the transaction, usually by solving a math equation that is complex, before they are rewarded with more of the Bitcoin. This process is called mining and is one of the ways that people can earn a lot of Bitcoin, but we will talk more about that later.

Bitcoin was developed in 2009, but very few people heard about it or used it at the time. The idea behind developing this kind of currency was to take control of money away from governments and central bankers, two groups that often manipulate money to their own personal gain. It is still unknown who exactly developed Bitcoin. The group Satoshi Nakamoto are recognized as the creators, but no one knows who is behind this group.

So, how does Bitcoin work? To start, you need to get the Bitcoin wallet app and have it on your phone or computer. There are several ways that you can then earn Bitcoin. If you would just like to make some purchases with Bitcoin, you can use your banking information to purchase or exchange for them. Some merchants will open up the wallet and start accepting Bitcoin for their goods and services. Others will invest, give money to start-up companies, or use the mining technique from before to earn more Bitcoin.

There are quite a few places where you are able to use Bitcoin, and that list is growing as more and more people want to use this online currency. Some big online merchants, like Overstock.com and OkCupid, will accept Bitcoin. Some car dealership allows you to use Bitcoin, like one in Southern

California who had a customer buy a Tesla Model S with their Bitcoins. Many people who are offering goods and services can list them online and will accept Bitcoin. If you want to purchase something with Bitcoin, you simply need to check out their website to see if this is an option.

So why is Bitcoin such a great option to work with? Some say that it is a good deal for a business, especially a small one, to accept Bitcoin. In most cases, these businesses would need to pay some sort of fee to the credit card companies each time that a customer uses a card to pay for something. This can get expensive for some companies. But with Bitcoin, the transactions are free and this could save the merchants a lot of money.

Bitcoin is also anonymous. While you will need to provide your banking information if you would like to exchange or purchase Bitcoin, all the information is encrypted and no one is able to trace it back to you. This makes it nice to protect against identity theft, though there are some people who use it to purchase items that may not be legal in their areas.

Bitcoin is also really secure. Through the process of mining, the transactions will all get a security code. Each number in the code is dependent on the next one, so if one number is changed, the rest of the code will change as well. This can help make it easier for a merchant to see if a transaction is legitimate or not before they send out their product.

And there are a lot of great companies that will let you shop with Bitcoin. Since it is not tied to a bank or a government agency, you can rest assured that the value isn't going to just suddenly drop out like it can with traditional money. This is a

*Chapter 1: What are the Differences Between Bitcoin and Ethereum*

sigh of relief for a lot of people, especially those who may have some turmoil with the banks right now.

## The split in Bitcoin

One recent change with Bitcoin is that the currency was recently split in two. Basically, the split has occurred because some of the ideological, technological, and political debates about how to grow Bitcoin have come together and forced it. One side of the split, which is known as Bitcoin Cash (BCH), is going to help scale up Bitcoin and make it easier for everyone to get a hold of it. There have been some growing pains with making this available to everyone, and some people believe that using the same software to create a brand-new currency is the best way to deal with this.

Over the years, Bitcoin has grown quite a bit and because of this, the blockchain that controls the transactions is becoming kind of congested and slowing down. For some, Bitcoin Cash seems to be the answer. BCH is novel software that will allow for eight times the amount of transactions on each block chain, helping to clear out some of the congestion that is there. However, the value of the Bitcoin in Bitcoin Cash could go down though. Bitcoin is worth about $ $3,461 each and the Bitcoin Cash would be worth around $313.70 (Jul 23, 2017).

Since these work similarly, other than the price of each will change and the process should be faster, what is this change going to mean for businesses and consumers who use the system? Anyone who already has Bitcoin is going to end up having the same amount of BCH. However, it is important to know that some of the exchanges that used Bitcoin are not going to accept Bitcoin Cash, which could be a bad thing for the potential spread of Bitcoin.

The hardest part of this process is getting businesses to start accepting it as payment. It doesn't matter so much what the changes are, though adding in more transactions to a blockchain will certainly help work out some of the kinks of Bitcoin. But if Bitcoin Cash is to become mainstream and be used for regular transactions, businesses need to be willing to accept it. This could take some time, but as more people want to use Bitcoin, it is likely that businesses will want to jump on as well.

## What is Ethereum?

Ethereum is another choice that you can use in cryptocurrency. This one is a bit newer than Bitcoin so it hasn't come up with quite as big of a following as that option, but it is still popular. There are some differences between these two currencies, though. For example, unlike the Bitcoin platform, Ethereum has been designed to be a smart contract platform which is also based on the blockchain technology.

The tokens for this cryptocurrency are available on a platform that is known as Ether. The ETH platform was designed specifically to be used for making any payment for hosting and accessing applications that are on the Ethereum blockchain. These apps will run on a blockchain, which is a powerful infrastructure that can be shared globally and which will move value around while also representing the ownership of that property. This can be created because it will allow the developers to create markets, move funds through the right

*Chapter 1: What are the Differences Between Bitcoin and Ethereum*

instructions, store their debts and promises in registries, and many other options. The best part is that all of these can be done without needing to add in a middle man.

The idea of Ethereum was released in 2014 by fans all around the world. This type of currency was developed by a company known as the Ethereum Foundation, which is a Swiss non-profit company, and there are contributions to this platform from all over the globe.

As you can see, Ethereum is a bit different and there are some limitations that come with this one that may not be seen with Bitcoin, but it is still a good option to work with. First, it is possible to work on mining inside of Ethereum as well in order to earn more of this cryptocurrency as well. If you have worked with Bitcoin in the past, you have seen how the mining can work. This process is when people who are already on the network will work on the codes that help maintain the applications and let them continue running. This process can also be used to start up new blocks on the blockchain and to go through and process the transactions that occur on the network. When the miners are successful, they will receive Ether, or the minted crypto-tokens, as their reward or payment.

Just like with the other cryptocurrencies, Ether has a value and you will be able to buy or sell them based on the current value of other types of cryptocurrencies. There are quite a few cryptocurrencies that are happy to do exchanges with Ethereum so it is easy to find the one that is right for you.

## The differences between Bitcoin and Ethereum

While both of these get their power by the principle of cryptography and distributed ledgers there are some technical differences in the two currencies respectively technologies. First of all, they differ regarding their programming languages. Ethereum is utilizing Turning while Bitcoin uses stack based languages. The block time is different as well. Ethereum is going to get done with transactions within a few seconds, but it does take longer when using Bitcoin. And the basic builds of these two currencies are different in the algorithms that they use.

But most people are not interested in these technical differences (other than the transaction time being faster is usually appreciated). The biggest difference that you are going to notice between these two is the purpose of using them. Bitcoin was designed to be an alternative to regular money. This means that you are able to use it in stores and in pretty much the same way that you do money, as long as the company accepts that form of payment. You get the added bonus of not having a bank or a government agency control the money. If you are looking for a safe, secure, and anonymous way to make purchases, Bitcoin is the right one for you.

On the other hand, Ethereum was developed as a type of platform that you would use to facilitate peer-to-peer contracts and applications with its own vehicle for currency. It is a way for people to get money to help create new applications, money that they would get from investors who are interested in the app. While Ethereum is a digital currency just like Bitcoin, the purpose is to monetize and facilitate Ethereum to

*Chapter 1: What are the Differences Between Bitcoin and Ethereum*

work so that developers are able to build and then run distributed applications.

In summary, while both of these work online and use the same idea of a blockchain, they are not even going to compete with each other. But since the Ether has gained a lot of popularity, it has become a competitor to many of the other cryptocurrencies, especially when looking at it from a trading perspective. For example, the market cap of the Ether is higher than Litecoin or Ripple but it still has a bit to go to reach Bitcoin. With that being said, both of these cryptocurrencies could be effective and popular at the same time, since they have different end goals.

In spite of the fact that Ethereum and Bitcoin may have comparative perspectives, the two monetary standards are altogether different as to the utilization as well as the eventual fate of the two digital assets. At the same time as the fate of ETH is vague there is an appealing investment opening to catch the potential expansion of the innovation. Concerning BTC, there is still space for development along with esteem; however, it won't be at the unstable rate it encountered in the commencement years.

# CHAPTER 2:

# Opportunities to Invest in Bitcoin (Classic and Cash) vs. Ethereum

**Direct investing**

The first type of investing, and often the one that is seen as the easiest right now, is to work with direct investing. What this basically means is that you will take your American Dollars (or the other currencies that you want to use) and then use these to purchase some of the cryptocurrency of your choice. Investors hold onto the cryptocurrency, not spending it or using it for anything else.

After a bit of time, the investor is going to exchange the cryptocurrency back for their original form of currency, such as the American Dollar. The point is that the cryptocurrency is going to gain value and then you will have more money. So, if the cryptocurrency that you picked out was worth $10, you would hold onto it for a bit (sometimes for a few years to make the most) and then when you sell, it may be worth $20. You can exchange out the Ether or the Bitcoin that you have in order to get it back in USD and make a profit.

This is a pretty basic form of investing, especially if you are going to stick with the investment for the long-term rather than switching right away. Both of these platforms have seen a lot of growth ever since they started and since it is predicted that they will grow you can easily make a big profit. However, you need to stick with it for the long-run. Like any other investment, there will be highs and lows over the short-term so this is not always the best option if you want to make money right away, but if you can wait it out for a year or so, this is a fantastic way to really see a return on investment.

There are many reasons why buying cryptocurrency could be profitable. Despite the fact that this currency did have a rocky start because it was a new idea, there are many retailers around the world, like Overstock and Microsoft, who already directly accept Bitcoin, and there are even ways to work around the problem with some of the retailers who don't. For example, you could use your Bitcoin to purchase gift cards that work on Amazon.

It is believed that proponents of cryptocurrency are going to keep on growing as time goes on. Cryptocurrency is fast and easy to use and many major companies are already using it. And as cryptocurrencies grow into new markets and become more widely accepted, the value of them will grow as well.

This is a good thing for the investor. As more and more people start to accept the value of cryptocurrency and it starts to be used in more companies the value is going to keep growing. While it has already increased quite a bit since it was developed and introduced, there is still a lot of potential throughout the world. It doesn't really matter which country you are from or which currency you use, Bitcoin goes all around the world. This opens up a huge market and if you start investing early on, you will see your money grow.

There are still some people who are wary about direct investing in Bitcoin or Ethereum options. While the price of these is going up, there are some that are worried because it can be almost impossible to figure out what a fair price for the Ether or Bitcoin will be. Part of what will make assets, including currencies, valuable is that they already have a history of appreciation, which cryptocurrencies have not had the chance to work with. Then there is also a problem with people not agreeing on the right rules for Bitcoin, which is why there has been the separation of Bitcoin in recent times.

And defining these currencies is hard, which can mean it impossible to figure out their value. Since a currency is something that is backed by the government, which cryptocurrencies pride themselves on not being, and they are not really stocks, they aren't going to report their earnings or generate a profit, two things that help others figure out a fair price for the currency.

Now, there are a few people who are working on formulas that will help consumers figure out what the Bitcoin fair price would be. But these conflict quite a bit. One financial analyst from London believes that the value of bitcoin is over 200 percent higher than it should be but there are some skeptics who believe that there really isn't any value in this cryptocurrency to start with.

The biggest issue that still surrounds these cryptocurrencies is that they are associated often with criminal activity. Since these currencies are all anonymous, it is easy for people to purchase items that are illegal or do things that are illegal without anyone being able to figure out who they are. This has put a bit of a shadow on the cryptocurrencies, but for the most part, people still like to use the currency and most people use it without having any criminal intentions.

## Chapter 2: Opportunities to Invest in Bitcoin vs. Ethereum

Bitcoin and Ether are great options to choose to invest in, you just need to understand what you are getting into. One of the biggest downfalls is that the currency is still new and many companies are not accepting it and that they do have kind of a criminal history behind them. But there is a rising popularity of this type of currency, which could mean a big profit for you. Just make sure that you watch the market and do your research instead of just jumping right in.

**Lending money to others**

Another option that you can choose to do with the Bitcoin and Ether is to become a lender. This is discussed a bit later in terms of lending out to startup companies through the ETH platform, but this method would be more to individuals. You can help them with a small business idea, but it would be more about helping with a small car loan or helping them with some bills and so on.

There are a lot of people who may need a little help with their bills or other things in life, but for one reason or another, they are having trouble doing it through a bank. If you have a few Bitcoin available, you may be able to make a bit of money and help someone out.

Before you lend the money, make sure to take a look at the background of the person you want to lend to. What are they going to use the money for, how much do they want to borrow, how long do they want to pay it back, and what are some of the reasons that the bank didn't give them the loan? If they are delinquent on five loans in the last few years, they probably aren't the best option, but if their credit score is a little low because they are young and haven't built it up, they may be fine.

Make sure that you and the borrower set up the rules of the transaction before getting started. You should set up how long they have to pay it off, how much they pay off each month, the interest rate, and what happens if they don't pay it back. Working with a smart contract can be a great idea because it ensures that both parties will be protected.

## Indirect investing

There are a few different types of investments that you can do that will help you make money off Bitcoin and Ethereum, but which won't require you to actually purchase the currency and hold onto it. Some of the options include funding a startup for an application that is on the Ethereum platform, investing in the Bitcoin and Ethereum companies, using smart contracts and more. Let's take a look at how these all work so you can make an educated decisions for your investing.

### *Investing in the company*

The first type of indirect investing opportunity that you can choose is to invest directly in the company. You will still not own any of the cryptocurrency with this, instead, you will invest in a way that helps the company to grow and do well. This is similar to what you would do when you join the stock market; you will pick out a company and then purchase bonds, stocks or other options that give you partial ownership of the company.

You will be able to pick how much you would like to invest into the company. This is generally considered a safe way to invest because these cryptocurrencies are growing like crazy and you have an actual tangible product that you are able to purchase and sell. You can choose what type of ownership you would like to have how much you want to spend, and more. Then every quarter, you will receive a profit when the company realizes profits based on the amount that you invested.

As long as the company is doing well, you are going to make a profit from this form of investing. You do need to watch the market to find out when the stocks are going up and when they are going down and plan your next move, but this is a really good long-term investment and it can become kind of passive. Since both Bitcoin and Ethereum are doing so well and they have such a large market that is still untapped, it is not likely they will see a decline anytime soon. You could easily put your money into the companies directly and see the money come back over the years.

## *Using Ethereum to fund a start-up*

Ethereum is quickly becoming one of the best places for tech start-ups to go when they need new funding. While this may have been done in Silicon Valley in the past, it is much easier to find this funding through the Ethereum platform. Many start-ups like this option because they are able to work on a platform that is distributed through the Internet, decentralized, and secure. And it has all of the ingredients that are needed so that a startup can get going without having to worry about their physical location.

To use this platform, users will have to use a liquid medium for value exchange, which is the Ether currency. They can also work with smart contracts, which is the common system for business and application logic through this system. To add to all of this, the Ethereum platform is great because it has developed a culture that is going to support and encourage innovation in the tech startup world.

Many new startups have moved over to this platform and have been able to sell their own 'tokens' to a globally distributed crowd of early adopters. These tokens are unique because they are cryptocurrencies that will have a special utility within a given application. In this case, the cryptocurrency is going to be used to help a startup get the funding they need to start and grow their business. For a project that is based on the Ethereum project, selling these tokens will solve two or three problems including:

It will provide the funding that the new company needs for their project.

It is going to bring together a new community of people who are excited, and who have an incentive, to get the application up and running.

It is a model of payment that can be used without having to worry about government or bank control.

This can be beneficial to the startup company and to the investor. The company is going to have a new way to start up their own business and get the funding that they need, without having to worry about going through the bank or another company to get the funding. This method is often easier and it can be nice to have a group of enthused people to help the project gain traction from the beginning, rather than just going through the bank.

The investor will also enjoy this as well. They will be able to find an application or a company that you are excited about and then can invest in them. You will be able to earn a profit when the company goes live or when the project is done, which will earn you money. And there won't be the constraints of banks and other investment options; you just require to work through the ETH platform and you will be set to go.

You do need to still do your research, though. There are quite a few startup companies that are using the Ethereum platform to help them grow their business or to start out a new project so there are many options for you to try out. But you do need to be careful. There will be some that are really good and some that are not that good.

While some of these options are going to be brand new to the world and may not have a bunch of research to show how they have done in the past, this doesn't mean that you can't do some research. It also doesn't mean that you should bypass these options. For these, make sure to get the information that you can. Take a look at the product, look at who runs the company, look at the business plan, and get the information that you can before you choose or give up on the investment. This can help you to determine whether the company has a good future or not.

***Start your own business***

It is possible to use these platforms to start your own business.

It would work similarly to how you would start a brick and mortar business, but you could keep it all online. There are really quite a few businesses who work on these platforms and the list is always growing. As long as you are able to provide services to others after accepting their cryptocurrency, you will be fine.

Some people decide to do a business completely online and then accept Bitcoin, Ethereum, and other cryptocurrencies as a form of payment. They can sell clothes, shoes, household appliances, and more. Then when they are all done, they can withdraw the currency into USD or another form of currency and use it how they would like. It is a pretty simple process and more companies are starting to add these on.

Even companies that don't offer services online are considering using Bitcoin as a form of payment. Grocery stores can accept Bitcoin by setting up a scanner that will take the money right from their customer's wallets. Some cleaning services, for example, could take these currencies online before the services. There are many ways that these cryptocurrencies can be used in helping you to start a new business or run an existing business.

### The use of smart contracts

No matter which option you choose to do with investing, it is a good idea to learn more about smart contracts. These are useful because they are going to help you to exchange shares, property, money, and anything else that has value in a way that avoids having a middle man and avoids conflict. In most cases, you would use a lawyer to do this and then pay them and a notary to get the contract done. With the smart contracts, you are able to drop some cryptocurrency into the ledger, and the smart contract will be done.

Considering a real life case it could look like this: you could rent an apartment using the blockchain that you paid for with the cryptocurrency. You are going to get a receipt when the transaction is done, which will be held in the virtual contract. The apartment owner needs to send you a digital entry key by a certain date, and if this doesn't come to you, the blockchain is going to release your money back to you. If the key is released, then the money will be sent to the other party. This helps both sides to be safe. If the key isn't released, you will get your money back, but if it is, the apartment owner is sure to get paid as well.

There are several ways that you can use these smart contracts. The first way is to use it when you make sales and purchases with other people through these sites. Since all these transactions are going to happen online, it is best to have some sort of safety feature to protect both parties. You are sure to get paid no matter what you do, and this keeps you safe.

If you have some computer knowledge, you can set up a system to create these smart contracts. The users of these contracts have to pay a few Bitcoin to make them work, so you could make a bit of money off each these transactions. You would need to be versed in coding to make the contracts and make sure that they are binding and working well, but it can be a way to make a second income.

## Mining

One popular option for those who want to make money with these currencies and who have some programming knowledge is the process of mining. In most cryptocurrencies (especially Bitcoin), there is a set amount of the currency available and there won't be any more that is ever made, unlike what we can find with most traditional currencies where the government can just make more. But when these currencies were released, they only released a certain amount. The rest need to be mined to be released.

Those who are able to do the mining business are going to be able to help not only themselves in this process but also other users. Remember that Bitcoin and Ethereum are used with a blockchain to help keep information safe and secure, but since it posts on a ledger, it needs to be done in a way that shows that the transactions have been completed. Both of these have a complex system for how these transactions should be stored, without giving away any information about either party.

For example, Bitcoin will have a series of numbers that will be related to each other. This means that if you change one number in the sequence, all the numbers that follow will change as well. There are many other rules to it as well, which is what will make mining so hard. If you are able to successfully complete some of these sequences though, you can earn money in Bitcoin so for programmers and computer buffs; this is the best option to use.

One of the big advantages of going with the indirect investments is that there are so many options that you can

*Chapter 2: Opportunities to Invest in Bitcoin vs. Ethereum*

choose from. You can really personalize the option and figure out what you like. You can choose to work on the contracts and on mining if you would like to stick with more of the programming stuff, you can start your own business, you can invest in a start up or do so many other things. The options are what makes these platforms so great to use.

The disadvantage is that you do need to do your research. These options are sometimes hard, like with mining, and you are not going to make money overnight. And with some of them, like with investing in a startup company, you may lose money, even though the Etereum platform is growing. You have to always be vigilant in what you pick out and make sure to protect your investment as much as possible.

**Mixed investments**

Doing a mixed investment is probably one of the best decisions that you can do with cryptocurrency investing. This allows you to split your money up between a few options in the direct investing and the indirect investing categories. This reduces the risk, helps you to get the benefits of each, and can bring in more money over time.

The idea behind this one is to not put all your money in one basket. Maybe you take some of your money and split it between investing in the Ethereum platform and the Bitcoin platform. Then you take some of your money and fund a startup and a few other companies. This helps you to spread out the money and keeps you safer than before.

If something does happen to one of your investment options, such as picking a startup company that doesn't do as well as expected, you still have some other investments pulling you up. You are likely to still make a profit, even though you lost a bit of money. But if you placed all the money in that investment that tanked, you would have lost out on everything.

There is no right or wrong mix of your investments to see the most money, but you should take a look around and pick out the one that you are the most comfortable with. This process is often known as diversifying your portfolio and it is one of the best techniques to make sure that you reduce your risk. All the best investors, whether they are working on cryptocurrencies or something else, will use this option because it helps to minimize their risks while maximizing their profits.

Beyond 2017, anything can come about. Indeed, even industry specialists can't precisely anticipate how exceptionally quick cryptocurrency expansion will wipe out. Plenty will rely upon whether autonomous countries take the Japanese route and distinguish them from genuine currencies or the German course and transparently show hawkish intents.

We would all be able to concur that the innovation is profitable and here to stay. The million-dollar question encompasses adoption. Will controllers around the globe grasp all the blockchain currencies as fiat measures up to, or will they regard them as antagonistic foes to their monopoly-based fiat frameworks?

## How to purchase & store cryptocurrency?

On the off chance that you have some play cash and need to make a gamble on cryptocurrency, you ought to completely feel 100% good with using up all that cash. Cryptocurrencies have collapsed some time recently, over and over again, and presumably will again later on. They're likewise generally costly in the event that you should get a few, you may be served by sitting tight a bit at costs to drop, so will probably get it. There are hordes of modes to purchase cryptocurrencies, and a few nations have even set up methods to buy them by means of an ATM.

Coinbase is amongst the extremely eminent Bitcoin agents and frequently prescribed for beginners. Coinbase permits you to purchase Bitcoin and different cryptocurrencies by connecting to your debit or credit card. Business Insider testifies that the mobile app is buggy, and banks will occasionally bolt a card subsequent to making these transactions. With that in mind, BI suggests telling your financial institution prior attempting to make a buy.

There are a couple of different choices; however, they have to a lesser extent a reputation: Kraken is one respectable option; it has been around since 2011 and works with an extensive variety of dealers & governments. There's likewise Gemini, yet it is not thus far accessible in each state.

Lastly, since trades, even the biggest ones, have smashed unexpectedly, it's additionally imperative to get yourself a protected place to store your Bitcoin, in the event that your supplier leaves the business or endures a hack. These tools are frequently alluded to as Bitcoin or cryptocurrency wallets. The wallet is, in fact, a physical gadget that interfaces with your PC and goes about as another source of defense. This implies you can't send Bitcoins from your wallet without possessing the physical gadget. There are so many of them such as:

## Hardware ledger wallets

- Ledger Bitcoin wallet
- Coinbase Bitcoin wallet
- TREZOR Bitcoin wallet
- Blockchain.info Bitcoin wallet
- Jaxx Bitcoin & Altcoin wallet
- Exodus Blockchain assets wallet
- MyCelium Bitcoin wallet
- Bitcoin Core wallet
- Keepkey Bitcoin wallet
- Electrum Bitcoin wallet
- Xapo Bitcoin wallet
- Armory Bitcoin wallet
- CoinKite Bitcoin wallet
- Bitcoin Wallet
- Green Address Bitcoin wallet
- Bitcoin Wallet
- BitGo Bitcoin wallet
- Copay Bitcoin wallet
- Airbitz Bitcoin wallet
- CoolWallet Bitcoin wallet
- BitLox

*Chapter 2: Opportunities to Invest in Bitcoin vs. Ethereum*

**Software based online ledgers**

SAP ERP

Sage 100c/300c/X3

MYOB

InFocus

Intacct

Acumatica

NetSuite ERP

Oracle Financials Cloud

FinancialForce

Goldenseal Accounting

Unit4 Business World

Traverse Cloud ERP

Microsoft Dynamics

In case you're earnest regarding crypto, obtain a hardware wallet. It doesn't become so clearer than this caption. Of course, hardware wallets cost cash and nobody loves to pay out money on items they can acquire for free. On the contrary, the measure of security you obtain by utilizing a hardware wallet is substantially more significant than the 50-$100 you'll pay for buying the genuine gadget. Don't say "it won't transpire" in light of the fact that once cryptocurrency progresses toward becoming standard (and it appears as though we're arriving really quickly) there will be numerous more instances of hacking or burglary. Ensure you're prepared...

## What About Alternatives?

One could contend it is similarly conceivable to put resources into vehicles, for example, GBTC. That investment alternative is additionally straightly connected to the Bitcoin esteem. That is unquestionably a substantial alternative, supposing you are an accomplished investor or financial investor. The normal individual in the city won't consider GBTC to be an essential alternative to any methods. Additionally, GBTC likewise gives access to Ethereum Classic, which isn't the equivalent as Ethereum. This may puzzle many people who aren't knowledgeable in the fine complexities of cryptocurrency right now.

Standard customers hoping to receive the benefits from Bitcoin's value additions should investigate BitcoinIRA. It is an amazing answer for individuals who need to procure cash as an afterthought without worrying. Furthermore, it is an extraordinary tool to develop a retirement fund. The Bitcoin cost will in all probability just go up more from here. BitcoinIRA is an available as well as a reasonable solution with a capability for high returns.

During 1999 the world perceived the IPO (speculative internet). These days, it's the ICO (initial coin offering). Organizations based on the blockchain, a digital database for recording monetary exchanges and different sorts of agreements, are boosting money by means of offering digital "tokens" that can characteristically be utilized to pay for goods & services on their platform or merely put away as an investment. Up to this point in 2017, organizations have brought $180 million up in ICOs, contrasted with $101 million all of a year ago, as per Smith + Crown, a blockchain research,

*Chapter 2: Opportunities to Invest in Bitcoin vs. Ethereum*

data and consulting group. Time and again, these are early tasks that are a long way from producing substantial income.

Enthusiasm for cryptocurrencies is achieving the majority. In the meantime, 10 monetary establishments joined with cryptocurrency platform Ripple just recently to send real-time international payments, joining a list of customers that by now included Bank of America & RBC. A definitive visualization is the world in which all data & transactions are detectable by means of an electronic ledger that wipes out hold-ups caused by divergent monetary standards and money related frameworks. Blockchain as of now claims to process 160,000 transactions per day crosswise over 140 nations.

Despite the fact that the vast majority of the folks purchasing Ether & Bitcoin are a singular investor, the advantages that both have encountered have taken what was in recent times a peculiar periphery try into the domain of huge cash. The consolidated estimation of all Ether & Bitcoin is currently worth greater than the market estimation of PayPal and is moving toward the span of Goldman Sachs.

**Various Other Significant Cryptocurrencies for Investing**

Litecoin (LTC)

Litecoin commenced in the year 2011, was amongst the underlying cryptocurrencies following Bitcoin and was regularly alluded to as 'silver to Bitcoin's gold.' Litecoin depends on an open source global payment network that is not controlled by means of any central authority and utilizes "scrypt" as an evidence of work, which can be decoded with the assistance of CPUs of consumer grade. Despite the fact that Litecoin resembles Bitcoin from numerous points of view, it has a speedy block generation ratio and consequently offers a speedier transaction affirmation. Other than developers, there are the greater numbers of merchants who acknowledge LTC.

Digital Cash (DASH)

Dash initially identified as Darkcoin is a more cryptic form of Bitcoin. Dash imparts greater obscurity as it attends to a decentralized mastercode network that formulates exchanges untraceable. Released to market in January 2014, Dash had a notable success and gained lots of supporters in a very short time. In March 2015, "Darkcoin" was rebreeding to Dash, which appears for Digital Cash and works under the ticker DASH. The rebuffing didn't transform any of its technological characteristics, for example, InstantX, Darksend.

Zcash (ZEC)

Zcash is decentralized & open-source cryptocurrency initiated in the last part of 2016, seems promising. On the off chance that Bitcoin resembles http for cash, Zcash is https, is the manner by which Zcash characterizes itself. Zcash offers privacy along with selective transparency of exchanges. Along these lines, similar to https, Zcash asserts to give additional security or protection where entire transactions are recorded and distributed on a blockchain, however particulars, for example, the sender, beneficiary, and sum stay private. ZEC offers its clients the option of shielded transactions, which take into account content to be encoded utilizing advanced cryptographic strategy or zero-knowledge proof construction known as a zk-SNARK created by its group.

## Monero (XMR)

Monero is safe, private & untraceable money. This open source cryptocurrency was propelled in April 2014 and shortly spiked incredible enthusiasm amongst the cryptography community and fans. The advancement of this digital money is totally donation-based & community-driven. XMR has been started with a solid core on decentralization plus expandability, as well as empowers complete privacy by utilizing an exceptional procedure described as ring signatures. With this strategy, there shows up a gathering of cryptographic signatures consisting of as a minimum one genuine member yet since they all seem legitimate, the genuine one can't be disengaged.

## Ripple (XRP)

Ripple is a real-time worldwide settlement network that tenders instant, definite and economical international payments. Ripple empowers banks to settle trans-border payments in real time, together with end-to-end transparency, and at reduced prices. Circulated in 2012, Ripple money has a market capitalization of $1.26 billion. Ripple's consensus ledger its strategy for adaptation needn't bother with mining, an attribute that diverges from Bitcoin as well as Altcoins. Seeing as Ripple's structure doesn't necessitate mining, it diminishes the utilization of computing power and limits network latency. Ripple trusts that distributing value is a commanding approach to boost certain practices and in this way as of now intends to disseminate XRP fundamentally in the course of business advancement bargains, inducement to liquidity suppliers who present extra tougher spreads for payments and selling XRP to institutional purchasers keen on putting resources into XRP.

# CHAPTER 3:

# The Rules of Serious Investing

When you are ready to get started in investing, whether you want to invest with cryptocurrency or some other option, it is important to take things seriously. It is tempting at times to go out there and just start investing and think that this isn't serious. Since most of the investing are going to happen on a computer and the idea of Bitcoin and Ethereum are so new, it is easy to think that you are playing with pretend money. But just like with other investments, you are dealing with real money that you can win or lose when working with Bitcoin and Ethereum and you need to take it seriously.

If you are ready to become serious about investing in cryptocurrency, it is important to understand where to get started. Here we are going to take a look at some of the best rules to remember when you are ready to get started with cryptocurrency investing.

**Markets return to the mean**

As you are looking at the market for Bitcoin or Ethereum, you will notice that there are some big highs and some big lows and many times when it is just in the middle. But no matter where the market has been at one point, it is always going to go back to the middle again. This can be really helpful to you when determining which investment to make.

For this one, you would need to take a look at some of the

charts that are available for the investment you are interested in. See where it is right now and then look to see where the mean is. If the investment is really high right now and is reaching about as high as it usually does, this means that it is going to go back to the middle pretty soon. This may not be the best option for you to pick right now because the investment will go down.

On the other hand, if you notice that the investment is lower than the average and has been there for a bit of time, this may be a good time to make a purchase. It is likely that the investment will go back up soon, and you will make a good amount of money.

## Excesses are never going to be permanent

It is sometimes hard for new investors to realize that their profits are limitless on one investment. Yes, you can keep going with investing and if you can move things around and make a lot of money, but each investment option is going to have some kind of limit to how much you can take in. While there are going to be sometimes when an investment, such as with Bitcoin or Ethereum, will skyrocket and make a lot of money in the process. But these trends are not going to be permanent. Instead, they will eventually return back to the mean. A smart investor will realize this and make some plans for when the reversal happens; a beginner will assume that these excesses will continue on forever and they will be burned.

## Chapter 3: The Rules of Serious Investing

**The public will buy the least at the bottom and the most at the top**

When you look at the average investor, you will find that there are some trends in the way that they make their investing decisions. These investors are often impressionable, innocent, and don't have the right counsel to help them make smart decisions. They may read the newspaper and pay attention to what they hear on TV, but they don't really know much about the market on their own.

The issue with this option is that by the time reporters tell the news about the market, the move has already occurred and a reversion has started, meaning that they have gotten some outdated information that can ruin their chances. This is why you as a good investor need to learn how to become a contrarian. Being able to do your own research and how to have independent thinking will serve you well. This helps you to make smart decisions that will get you ahead, rather than following the advice from outdated and uninformed sources.

**Avoid greed and fear**

What this one basically means is that you need to use your head, rather than your emotions, when making investing decisions. It doesn't matter if you are using cryptocurrencies or other forms of investing, the second that you let those emotions get the better of you is the moment that you will lose out on any profit that you hope for. These basic human emotions are going to be the biggest enemy that you try to be successful in investing.

If you want to see success with any type of investing that you choose, you need to learn how to make level-headed and disciplined decisions You have to look at your resources, watch the market, and make decisions based on your strategies. Your emotions should never factor in. There are too many times that people will get out of the market when there is just a tiny dip because they are afraid of losing everything, but then a few days later they find out they missed out when the market goes skyrocketing, in addition, there are people who avoid their strategy and keep going with the market because they want to make more profit, and they miss out when the market suddenly goes down.

The market will have these ups and these downs, but if you have a good strategy in place ahead of time, you can avoid some of these issues. You have to know when it is actually time to get out of the market, both when the market is up and when it is down, rather than just running away because you are scared of where the market is going or you become greedy and want to make more. The market will always turn around so having a strategy and an exit plan for every investment will help save you.

## When the experts all agree, go the opposite way

There are a few times when the forecasts and the experts all agree that one thing or another will happen. But this is usually a time when you need to be on alert. It usually means that the market for that trend has become saturated and that everyone in the market who will purchase that investment has already made purchases. It means there are no longer any buyers. Once this happens, the market must go lower so that someone new will make a purchase, since there are likely to be many sellers and very few, if any buyers.

It can also go the other way as well, so always be careful when all the sources start to agree. They will often fall behind and if you go by this advice, especially when the forecast and the experts all agree, you may find that you make the wrong decisions.

**Watch for the three stages of the bear market**

What some new investors don't understand is that all markets are going to have stages and learning these stages will help you to figure out whether it is the right time to get into the market or not. This is true even when you are dealing with cryptocurrency. When you are working with a bear market, there will be a sharp downward turn, a rebound when some new buyers think the market will get better, and then the downtrend is drawn out a bit more.

A bear market doesn't mean that you shouldn't invest. There are still plenty of investments that do well in these markets, you just need to make sure that you pick out the right option. And this is where cryptocurrencies can come into the mix. These have all done well, and while they do have some ups and downs on occasion, they have not had the bad markets that some of the other stock markets have. But even in the stock market, you will find some investments that do well even in a bear market so just do your research and look around for the best option.

## Have your own strategy

There are lists and lists of strategies that you can read about online and in books and many of them are great resources to help you come up with your own strategy. But no matter what these books say, you need to create your own strategy. And since both Bitcoin and Ethereum are new forms of investing, you can have a lot of fun coming up with your own strategy to really see success.

You have to come up with a strategy that is going to fit you. If you like to look at charts and go with trends, this is a good option. If you want to take a look at the company and do a fundamental analysis, then go ahead and do this. The most important thing is that you find a strategy that you are comfortable with and that you stick with it. The biggest reason that people fail in investing of any kind is that they just weren't able to stick with their strategy and kept hopping around.

Getting into investing can be hard, no matter what kind of market you are working in. But understanding the topic that you want to go with, such as picking a company you like, backing up a product you feel passionate about, or something else, is so important when you want to see success. Stick with some of the rules that we discussed in this chapter, and you are sure to see results in all of your investment options.

## Invest with others

One way to help reduce some of the risks that you are dealing with is to combine your assets and invest with others. Sometimes you may not have the money needed to get started, such as when you want to help a new startup. Most people don't have that much money and they don't want to put in that much risk when starting out. When you combine together with other investors, you can still get in on the investment without having to lose out on everything if it fails.

This works kind of like a mutual fund. The investors can all share the risks, but they also share the profits too. If you don't have enough money to get in on an investment by yourself, this is a good way to start out. If the company does well, you will earn a percentage of the profit based on how much you invested. But if they do poorly, you will lose some money, but that is shared as well. It is a safe way to build up your portfolio and to start earning money in cryptocurrency.

# CHAPTER 4:

# How to Reduce Your Risks with These Investments

As a new investor, you want to make sure that you are decreasing your risks as much as possible. Any investment is going to have some risks, but if you jump into the investment without doing your research or coming up with a strategy, you are more likely to fail. There is a reason that some people make a lot of money in cryptocurrency and others fail quickly. This chapter is going to take a look at some of the easy things that you can do to help decrease your risks while working with Bitcoin and Ethereum.

**Diversify your portfolio**

One of the best things that you can do no matter what kind of investment you choose, is to diversify your portfolio. As a beginner, you may be excited about getting into the market and making some of your first investments. You want to jump into it all with two feet, but there are some issues that can come with this. You may be busy thinking about all the profit you can make when you put all your money into one investment. But what most investors don't think about is what happens if that investment does poorly.

If you put all of your money into one investment, you are increasing your risks quite a bit, even in an investment that is relatively safe. If that investment starts to do poorly, you will lose out on all your money and will have to restart from square one, which can be hard on many new beginners. Any investment can take a turn for the worse at times, many times due to factors that you can't control so it is best to plan for this.

To avoid this from happening, it is best to diversify your portfolio. What this means is that you take the money that you would like to invest, and put some of it into a few different investments. A number of investments that you can split your money between will depend on how much you have available, but the more times you split it up, the safer your money is.

The nice thing about this option is that even if one stock does poorly, you will only lose a little bit of money instead of all your money. And it is likely that at least one or more of your other options will increase in profit. You are much more likely to see a nice profit from your options when you split it up a bit, rather than putting all your money in one place.

**Invest in what you know**

Getting started in Bitcoin and Ethereum can be tough. It is a new adventure and you want to make sure that you are doing it the right way, but there are so many options and you may not be all that familiar with it. The best thing that you can remember is to invest in something that you know about.

Both of these currencies have a lot of options for you to choose from so there is sure to be something that you are knowledgeable about. Perhaps take some time to look through the Ethereum platform and see which apps are about things you know. While there are a lot of great apps and programs that will become available, you need to make sure that you are picking out something that you have some idea about. You can choose an industry that you are familiar with if that helps. When you know about the industry or the product, you are better able to tell if it is the best option for you to choose.

This can happen with Bitcoin as well. You want to make sure that you don't jump into something that you are completely confused about no matter which option you choose. Let's say that you like to go hunting and fishing. There may be an app or a company that sells these products and you can invest in them. If you are knowledgeable about another type of industry or company, consider going with those.

It is tempting to jump into a company or another investment because it looks like it is doing well, but if you know nothing about that industry or that investment, you are going to run into some trouble. You won't be able to pay attention to the news or what is going on around you, and you will end up doing poorly in the long run. Stick with what you know; even in the new cryptocurrency market, you are sure to find something that you know about.

**Keep your emotions out of the mix**

One of the most important things that you can do when working with Bitcoin or Ethereum is to keep your emotions out of the game. These two options are brand new investments, which can be both exciting and scary. It is scary because there isn't a lot of information about these investment types since it is so new. But there is also some excitement since there are so many possibilities that can come with this option.

It can be hard to keep your emotions out of the game though, especially for someone who is new. There are times when you may put your money into the investment choice and then the market takes a downward turn right away. Usually, these are going to be pretty small and if you keep your money in for a little bit longer, you will end up making all that money back and more. But most people get a bit scared and freaked out, and then they withdraw their money. This results in a loss that could have easily turned into a gain if they didn't let their emotions get in the way.

This can happen to go the other way as well. Some people get so excited when they see that their investment is making money. They see it go higher and higher and they assume those highs will just keep on coming. But at some point, the investment will go down again to reach that mean. And if you hold onto your asset for too long you will see all those potential profits go down the drain. Once the market turns, it turns quickly and you can quickly lose out on everything because you got too excited.

Keeping your emotions out of the mix is the best thing that you can do. Make sure that you set up a strategy that tells you when to enter the market and when to leave will help to take some of the emotions out. This helps you to make smart decisions and then when one of the points of your strategy is met, whether it is the high point or the low point, you will leave and reduce your risk. Never let those emotions get in the way of you making good money on your investments.

**Do your research**

Since Ethereum and Bitcoin have not been around for a long

time, the amount of research that you can do about their investment options is a bit more limited compared to other options on the stock market. But this doesn't mean that you shouldn't do your research ahead of time. There is always going to be some research, no matter how recent the company is, that you can use to get the results that you want.

With Bitcoin, many people are choosing to just purchase the digital crypto coins and hold onto it to make a profit later when the prices rise. But there is still a good amount of research that you can do. You need to have a good idea of how much Bitcoin actually costs, how much it will rise in value in the future compared to your method of paying out (how much the Bitcoin is worth per American Dollar, for instance), and how much you should purchase. Researching the trends in Bitcoin and its value in different currencies can help you to make this decision.

Ethereum is a bit different and you will often work with apps and other startups instead of just investing in the currency, although that is an option as well. Get as much information about these apps and companies before starting. You want to make sure that they are going to grow their business well and won't just tank or take your money and run. If you are uncertain about where to start, talk to someone who has worked in these investment options and ask lots of questions to help you out.

**Keep some savings on hand**

No matter which of these two options you choose to go with, it is important that you always keep some savings on hand.

*Chapter 4: How to Reduce Your Risks with These Investments*

When you put all of your money into the investment, you could end up in trouble if the market goes down. Having some savings on hand, especially savings that is in cash, can help you out because it ensures that you are set in case something does go wrong.

Many new investors don't think about this step, and so they will invest all of the money that they can, not thinking about what will happen to them if all that money disappears. It is best to choose a comfortable amount that you would like to invest and stick with that. You may not make as much profit as you could this way, but you at least won't lose as much as you could either.

**Never invest money you don't have**

This is a big beginner's mistake that you have to avoid. It is tempting to look at some of the numbers that have come on the market with Bitcoin and Ethereum and to just throw all your money right at it. But no matter how well these cryptocurrencies have done, they still have some dips and if you don't invest wisely, you could end up losing your money.

The best method for investing is to only invest the amount that you are comfortable and willing to lose. Don't take out your retirement, don't use all your life savings, and don't take out a crazy loan to pay for this investment. Only use money that if you lost, you would still be fine afterward. It is tempting to do a big investment to see a big return in the process, but the market can easily turn the other way and you could lose out on everything.

## Know when to give in

No matter which way the market is going, it is important for you to know when it is time to give up. Actually this could be very tough to learn. There are times when you need to ride the market, even when it goes down a bit, but then there are times when you need to cut your losses and then move on to your next choice. Even when the market is going up, too. Yes, you may see that the market for that investment keeps creeping up, but at some point, the market will go back to the middle and if you don't learn the right time to get out, you will end up losing money instead of gaining.

One of the best ways to make sure that you don't go too far in either direction is to set an exit point. This is the point when you will get out of the market, no matter what it might do when you are done. You can set a low and a high exit point. So when the investment hits your low point, you will cut your losses and call it good. But when the investment hits the high point, you will withdraw and keep your earnings. There will be times when you miss out on some profit when the market goes above your exit point, but it is a lot better than losing out.

The point of doing this is to help you take your emotions out. As soon as those emotions get into the mix, you are going to take things too far and end up losing money. Set the points that you are comfortable with right from the beginning. If Bitcoin or Ether(eum) ends up going higher, you can always enter the market later on, but this will prevent you from losing too much money.

While any type of investment is going to be a risk, there are steps that you can take to minimize these risks a little bit.

*Chapter 4: How to Reduce Your Risks with These Investments*

Learning how to mix up your portfolio a bit so you have different options (in case one doesn't work out that well for you), taking the emotions out of the game, and coming up with a good investment strategy is one of the best ways for you to see success.

# CHAPTER 5:

# Best Strategies for Mid- and Long-Term Success with Cryptocurrency Investing

Investing in cryptocurrencies can take some time and research. While it would be nice to just jump into the process and make all that money right away, this is not really a valid option with any investment that you want to use. You need to know what you are talking about, have some ideas of what to invest in, and be ready for the long term. For example, just because there is a little dip in your investment right after you purchase or buy in doesn't mean that the investment won't do well. You just need to wait for it out a bit longer, and with some patience, you will see the profit that you want.

And this is the most important thing that you need to remember when it comes to investing in cryptocurrencies. Stay committed for the long term. These currencies are new but rising in popularity. This means that they have a lot of room to grow as more people start to use these currencies. If you can stick with it for the long term, you are sure to see huge results.

This chapter is going to spend some time looking at the best investing strategies that you can use in order to see success over the long term with cryptocurrency.

**Watch for the mean**

## Chapter 5: Best Strategies for Mid- and Long-Term Success

We talked about this one a bit earlier, but it is important to always look out for the mean. While some companies do increase in value over time, especially when inflation happens, they never see a big increase that stays the same and never goes back down. The increase in value is going to happen slowly over time, and you should be able to see this in the charts.

This means that you should always assume that the market of a company or investment, once it has gotten through some of the growing pains in the beginning, will go back to the medium at some point. There will be times when it goes up and you can make a lot of money and there are times when it may go down and you will lose a lot of money, but it should always go back to the middle. Knowing this, and taking the time to find this mean, will make it easier for you to make smart decisions with your investing.

For example, let's say that you get the charts from a company you are interested in investing in. You look and find out that the mean seems to be about $10 a share. Now, let's say that the shares are around $6 a share right now and that seems to be the point where the market turns around and the shares go back to the mean or above. This is good news for you if you make a purchase. You can get the shares for a good price and then earn money as they try to get back to the middle.

You can use the same logic when you are ready to sell the shares. For example, let's say that the shares are now worth about $12 each and the market doesn't usually let it get higher than that. You can choose to sell these shares now, before the market goes down, making a good profit in the meantime.

There are times when the market will go away from the normal and you could end up making more or losing more than this method allows for, but this one will help you out most of the time if you stick with it for a long enough time. Riding out the market for the long-term is a great option because you won't be affected by the rises and falls of your investment.

## Pick an app that is seeing some success

When you are working with Ethereum, you are going to look at a startup company or an app and then choose which one you would like to invest in. This means that you do need to have a good idea of what is going to do well. Looking for an app that is doing well is a good place to start though. If the app is already doing well can show that customers are already interested in it and the company may just need a few more investors to get results. This doesn't have to be a company that is already making a ton in profits, but there should be some popularity growing with it.

There need to be a few options that you look at before picking the app. First, look to see which apps are starting to gain a small following. This is where you will start, but take a look at the product and the company as well. Is there room for the app or the product to grow? Sure it may be doing well now, but if there is just one product and it can't be changed or modified in any way, the market will become saturated before long and it may not be the best long-term strategy. And if the company is already having trouble distributing the product or getting along, they will likely fail when things get tough.

This is why it is always so important for you to take a good look at the investment that you want to go with. Make sure that you don't just look at the charts, although this is a good place to get started. You also need to look at the potential for the company, how it is managed, and other factors to make sure you are picking out the best option.

**Do a fundamental analysis**

Another thing that you can do is a fundamental analysis of the company. This one is really useful with the Ether currency because you may not always have a lot of history to go from since this is a new form of currency. With the fundamental analysis, you won't really concentrate as much on the charts for the company, but on the company itself.

For this one, you are going to take a look at the management that is running the company, if there have been any major changes recently, what kind of product they plan to sell and if their research is sound, and so on. Applying this fundamental research could help you figure out whether the company is on the right track or not. There are many times when the company may have a rough start or when the economy drags it down a bit, but the company itself is solid and will do well.

On the other hand, there are companies that may do well when they first start out, but there may be something wrong within the company. They may change up the product, have a change in management, or have something else going on that could shake the industry trust in them. Their charts may look good, but there may also be a time soon when the company starts to see a loss in profits.

The fundamental analysis may not always help you to pick out the right company, but it is often more accurate than simply looking at the charts. Many people who purchase products and services from a company won't look at the charts, they will look at a company so this is a good place to start to pick out your investment.

## Buy and hold

This is a method that has been really popular with Bitcoin. Because it is easy to buy and trade out Bitcoin, there are some people who are willing to give up their bitcoins right when there is a little dip in the market. They will panic and assume that they are going to lose out on all the money they put in, so they try to get out of the market at the first sign of something going wrong.

The thing with Bitcoin is that it is going upwards at a nice and steady trend. Yes, there will be some little dips that occur, but for the most part, you are going to see that the value just keeps going up, especially as more people start to use Bitcoin to make their purchase. Unless you need to take the money out to make a purchase right away, it is best to just hold onto your Bitcoin and let the market grow.

Research has found that those who made the most out of investing with Bitcoin were the ones who stayed calm when things went down a bit and held onto the money. Yes, there are times when both the price of Ethereum and Bitcoin has gone down a bit, but there are way more times when their prices skyrocketed. Over the long term, it is best to hold onto the Bitcoin that you purchase for investing. This will help you to catch onto the rising tide, rather than missing out just because there was a little dip in prices for a day to two.

# Conclusion

Thank you for making it through to the end of this book, let's hope it was informative and able to provide you with all of the information you need to achieve your goals, whatever they may be.

The next step is to pick out which investment you would like to work with. Having a combination of Bitcoin and Ethereum investments can help you to diversify your portfolio and make the most money possible with your hard work. This guidebook will provide you with all the information that you need in order to get started with investing in these up and coming markets.

Many people are still new to the idea of cryptocurrency since they were all developed recently. And actually this is good news for you. Since it is just starting to gain popularity around the world, there is a lot of money to be made and getting in now, with some smart investment choices, can make this a good long-term investment opportunity. This guidebook will talk about some of the investments that you can choose that will help you get started.

When you are ready to expand out your portfolio or you want to get started on a smart method for investing, make sure to read through this guidebook and learn all the tips that you need to see results.

Finally, if you found this book useful in any way, your review on Amazon is always appreciated!

www.ingramcontent.com/pod-product-compliance
Lightning Source LLC
Chambersburg PA
CBHW050022230526
45470CB00003B/1083